also by pattiann rogers

Song of the World Becoming:
New and Collected Poems, 1981–2001

The Dream of the Marsh Wren:
Writing as Reciprocal Creation

A Covenant of Seasons

Eating Bread and Honey

Firekeeper: New and Selected Poems

Geocentric

Splitting and Binding

Legendary Performance

The Tattooed Lady in the Garden

The Expectations of Light

generations

pattiann rogers

penguin poets

PENGUIN BOOKS
Published by the Penguin Group
Penguin Group (USA) Inc., 375 Hudson Street,
New York, New York 10014, U.S.A.
Penguin Books Ltd, 80 Strand,
London WC2R 0RL, England
Penguin Books Australia Ltd, 250 Camberwell Road, Camberwell,
Victoria 3124, Australia
Penguin Books Canada Ltd, 10 Alcorn Avenue,
Toronto, Ontario, Canada M4V 3B2
Penguin Books India (P) Ltd, 11 Community Centre, Panchsheel Park,
New Delhi - 110 017, India
Penguin Books (N.Z.) Ltd, Cnr Rosedale and Airborne Roads, Albany,
Auckland, New Zealand
Penguin Books (South Africa) (Pty) Ltd, 24 Sturdee Avenue,
Rosebank, Johannesburg 2196, South Africa

Penguin Books Ltd, Registered Offices:
80 Strand, London WC2R 0RL, England

First published in Penguin Books 2004

10 9 8 7 6 5 4 3 2 1

Page 116 constitutes an extension of this copyright page.

LIBRARY OF CONGRESS CATALOGING-IN-PUBLICATION DATA
Rogers, Pattiann, 1940–
Generations / Pattiann Rogers.
p. cm.
ISBN 0-14-200450-2
I. Title.

PS3568.O454G46 2004
811'.54—dc22   2003064750

Printed in the United States of America
Set in Bembo
Designed by Ginger Legato

For my grandchildren, John Saurav Rogers
and Abraham Rockford Gillar Rogers

and for their fathers and for their mothers

contents

the first story

3/ Generations

5/ Keeping Up

7/ Jacob's Ladder

9/ Aspiring, Now and Then

11/ Creating a Pillar to Heaven

13/ Oh Mother, Oh Father (I Dream We Are Cats Beneath
Falling Leaves in an Autumn Wind)

15/ And Motion in Philosophy

17/ In Union: Skinny Grandfather Riding a Bicycle

19/ A Traversing

the second story

23/ Feeding Our Ancient Ancestors

25/ Symbols and Signs

27/ The Character of the Bowl

29/ Alpha and Omega

31/ The History of Starlight at Night

33/ Pilgrims, Missionaries, and Seers Visit *Heterocephalus glaber*

35/ The Lost Creation of the Earth

37/ Truth and Falsehood

38/ A Meeting of the Ways

39/ The Passing of the Wise Men

the third story

43/ The Soul of Subtlety

45/ In Another Place

47/ The Questing

48/ Seeing What Is Seen

50/ A Mystic in the Garden Mistakes Lizards for Ghosts
and Extrapolates on Same

52/ Tabula Rasa
54/ This Little Glade, Remember
56/ Into Their Own

the fourth story
61/ The Match
63/ God and His People
65/ Genus *Whistler*
67/ Servant, Birthright
69/ Ventriloquist
71/ Bearings on a Winter Evening
73/ The Body and the Soul

the fifth story
77/ In General
79/ On the Eve of the Hearing
81/ In the Terrace Garden
83/ Mischief in the Madrigal
84/ Interdisciplinary Studies
86/ From a Simple Vanilla Vortex Come Voices of the Faithful
88/ Come, Drink Here
89/ Another Principle in the Plot
91/ Watching the Living
93/ Gehenna

the following story
97/ The Ease of Murder
98/ Into the Wind's Castle
100/ The Measure of a Finger
102/ Grief
103/ Where God's Grief Appears
105/ A Statement of Certainty
107/ Fact Compounded: Stray Cat, Black and White
109/ Study from Right Angles
110/ Breaking Old Forms
112/ Beyond Redemption: the Precedent
114/ Who Might Have Said

generations

**t h e
f i r s t
s t o r y**

They have been walking from the beginning,
through the foggy sponges of lowland
forests, under umbrella leaves, in the shattered
rain of ocean beaches, through the tinder
of ash pits, the thickets of cities, along washes
and ravines and the dust of dry creek beds.

When the great ice mountain split
its continent and became two, they were walking.
When smoke from the burning plains
blinded the western seas, they were walking.
They walked by dead reckoning on steel,
on ropes, over swales and fens, on pearls.

They passed through congregations
of meteors, through knots of flies,
and howling tangles of hungry winds.
When they were sleeping on moss,
they were walking. When they lay
broken, torn and still on the field,
they were walking. They were walking
when the sun gathered together the tightening
strings of its slack, when the sun dissolved
into the withering circle of its power.

An old dog trailed them off and on,
and flocks of ricebirds and their shadows
rose up and scattered before them. Herds
of holy caribou and hosts of preying
wolves disappeared ahead of them
over the snowy hills. They were walking
with ghosts, with choirs of grasses
and armies of stars. They walked
through the words *let there be light*
more than once. They were walking

with chronicles of chains. They walked beyond
the headwaters of the moon.

And people saw them coming and people
saw them passing, and their walking
was constant, unmoving, invariable,
and the seeing of the people was ever
present, immutable, liberation.

Any faithful attendant must be able
to travel as fast as winds in a black
blizzard, as winds in the gales
of a north sea storm, must move parallel
with the cheetah, the coyote, the hare
and fleeing gazelle, must fall swiftly,
side by side with everything that falls—
rains, and meteors, and forests afire,
wounded men, crumpling cities,
melting mountainsides of snow.

Whatever monitors stone and fire
must circle the sun with the disintegrating
comets, the cold planets and their lackey
moons, orbit the galaxy with each and every
one of its stellar systems and bursting stars.

Whatever is steadfast must be
as quick as an electron moving by no
means across the emptiness between
one phantom ring and another, like a firefly
that loses its vanishing place and finds it
again across a vacancy of night.

To be in union with the seasonal,
that which adheres must go and return
year after year among winters and springs
with all of their motions multiple, speed
one by one with the flying spores of royal
ferns, with mescal beans flung outward
and each red, wind-spinning key
of the swamp maples, hover among
the migratory grey and the humpback
whales and the rapidly sailing spray

porpoises, matching eye to eye exactly
their true directions, their determined paces.

Whatever it is that keeps careful watch
with the fleet, the rapid, the brisk,
the headlong rising or descending,
must become itself the virtue
of velocity, the intimate of light.

Regard these immortal beings
as one by one they descend
in garments of scarlet tint like
evening shining on ivory terns
and ice-filled seas. They come
covered in seamless cloaks
like rain swaying like human ghosts
gathering across the prairie, in silver
sheen like salmon at night through
a black rush of rapids, come
veiled in laces like tall grasses
in webs of bowl and doily spiders,
like morning in a dispensation
of white-threaded poplar seeds.

Observe these immortal beings
step by step, scarves wrapped
around their presence like light
wrapped around field sunflowers
in full bloom. They descend
in rings and green drapery like
the birch and the sweet bay descend
without moving from their highest
branches down to the earth. Down
they come in ritual procession,
in hoods of violet velvet so
deep their faces disappear like
the faces deep inside the hoods
of monkshood blossoms disappear.

Watch them descend one by one
in robes of wind like silk flags
alive on their bones, dressed
in stars like shawls settled
like memory across their shoulders,
becoming the place of themselves
like descending mizzle sheathing

winter in glass, clothed like blue
Arctic butterflies in the eternal
form of their own motion. Arrayed
in the phenomena of immortality,
they are made immortal. Regard
these beings from heaven forever
in their earthly descent.

The spiral staircase in this tower
winds upward in tight circles.
I can hear each of my footsteps
as I go around and up on the worn
stones, the railing certain and cold
in my hand. I climb around
and around almost circling myself
in this narrow space, almost
meeting myself face to face,
one step behind, one step ahead.

I've climbed similar staircases
before, ascending windowless
cathedral towers up to high-wind
belfries where birds swoop and circle,
up to walkways of sudden sun
shining on red-tiled rooftops.
Once I climbed stairs leading
to a lamp twice as tall as a man,
brighter than 10,000 candles, a rotating
beacon at the top of a lighthouse
tower. The sea below was a rage
of contradiction and unanimity.

Old church towers often house gears
and cogs and spinning parts,
the operating machinery of enormous
clocks, crown wheels and click wheels
that creak and turn making minutes,
hammers that lift slowly and strike
making hours by sound. Climbing
to the top, one might touch the great
passing noise and workings of time.

There's a miracle staircase, a spiral
hanging in the desert suspended midair,

witnessed only in late autumn light
after dusk, before stars. I may have
seen it, though I have never climbed it.

Maybe the tower of Babel
had a spiral staircase too, maybe
just a wooden ladder the final
few steps to heaven for those who might
climb to the top without dizziness,
without falling in confusion.

Now and then someone might imagine
rising at night to enter its sheer black
tower of windows, imagine walking
through the doorway to climb the tight
galactic spiral. Circling its form, one
step ahead, one step past, the body might
discover and become by that motion alone
the grand inevitability of the galaxy itself.

Start anywhere . . . a ragged minstrel
dances with a fiddle round and round on the back
of a sleeping black cat;
                              a stick balancing
a spinning plate is poised on his greasy
head
        upon which spinning plate Death
in white stands tiptoe holding a golden
jack-o'-lantern by both hands
                              above her gorgeous
upturned, turning face,
                              atop which leering
lantern a cracked and ancient blue bowl
tips and sways;
                      a mountain of earth, seeds
of wild grasses, and a riley river fill the deep
blue of the gyring bowl
                              in which vesseled
soil an ancient oak roots itself
                              with hooks
and nails through cycles of summer;
                                      a glass
egg, holding the heart of a pulsing sun
and a skeleton of stars spinning inside
its oval surfaces, lies
                      in its nest clasped
high in the encompassing brackets of the oak's
uppermost branches;
                      and see, a black cat
is sleeping inside that egg, dreaming of weaving
through a sleek forest of sun-seeded grasses
as easily as a minstrel wind,
                              as poised
as Death beneath the nebulous sky within
and without the egg lying
                              secure in the steady
bowl of the nest and its retinue revolving round

and round to the refrain
                                    of a dizzy fiddler
laughing as if there were
                                    a detectable way
it could all have been meant to be forever.

oh mother, oh father
(i dream we are cats beneath falling
leaves in an autumn wind)

Sailing bird skeletons, entire
or in bone pieces, miracle bodies
filled with light, all those skittery
hearts and open wings are finally
set free now, falling from the sky.
They spiral and roll, bobbing
and swaying as if floating on the current
of a wide and ancient river.

Down they come within easy reach
of even the crippled, the scarred,
the one-eyed and the toothless,
the wretched and imbecilic. Even
the cockeyed, off-key leaping
of the insane is rewarded.

A flock of surrender, they weave
and twist in their falling, turning
sensually, tauntingly, exactly
as we always wished, a crowd
into which the homeliest among us
might bury himself, sink away,
become one with the delectable.

A few attempt escape, flee
in awkward wheels across the lawn,
a welcome chase, each easily captured
and kept. We pull them close.
They partner with us.

Some we catch are certain to contain
that luscious blood honey so magical,
so coveted. We might pierce, tap
and drink. We can taste it now.
Others, tumbling in mouse-like

curls, hold our loves that never were.
We call them our ardent hope.
They have experience with the skies.

Nestled deep inside any of these
wizened bodies, little lizardy bodies,
lies our most precious fear. We guard it.
We swallow it whole.

How could we have known before?
The spirit of heaven is a wind
made real by the illusions it carries.
Even the warriors among us
are satisfied without murder
over and over again.

We say we move miles across desert
ice and black volcanic sand, down
numbers of leagues into the night
of oceans and caves. Marking
units and distances, we say we move
an hour among damp spring grasses,
two days along canyon roads
and creek beds, country lakeside
borders. This is the way we move,
because we pronounce this to be
the way of our moving.

But maybe in truth we pass through
not just miles of forest but a testament
of trees, neither walking nor riding
but moving as sunlight moves in one
steady procedure through underwater
weeds or as music moves making
time and space of the void.

And perhaps we move as well
through ardor, entering it and leaving
as if it were an incendiary city
with gates. Perhaps we cross the seven
parameters of bliss as if each
were a slow river of meadow to ford.
In bed asleep we might approach
a settlement of inner union where
it exists in a thousand definite
coordinates around the earth.

All facts of the body, we know,
are composed solely of light
and its speed. Therefore, a traveling
beam of luminous star and a single blood

corpuscle of radiance in the heart must be,
in myth and song, one and the same.

While considering the consecrated
motion of winter moonlight across
a vision of white in the mind, it might
be possible to journey there, to move
at will with the conscious speed of prayer
through such a current of god.

1.

Grandfather and bicycle move together
down the gravel road, passing through
the two-dimensions of shadows and shades
melding and flickering over the single
being of their creaking, rattling motion.

In silhouette it would be impossible
to tell where the skinny old man's pipe-thin
arms actually stop and the handlebars
of the bicycle begin, both the same bent
shape and stiff intention.

The rhythmic click of his joints
as he slowly pumps the pedals matches
the click of the chain on the teeth
of the gears. Both skeletons
show their thin and bony frames.

2.

His feet circling with the pedals,
the turn of the wheels and spin of the rims,
spokes flashing in streaks as they catch
the light—this is a universe of heart centers,
hubs, covenants and revolutions proceeding on
in their ways as every universe does.

3.

The bicycle seems strangely out of breath now.
The tires groan on the gravel. They hesitate,
lurch ahead. Is it the grandfather panting?
Tensions strain and gasp.

The road turns suddenly, the bicycle
swerves, they veer too far, wobble wildly
close to catapulting into the ditch. Dust

flies, grasshoppers and field birds flee
in all directions. There are jagged
cries and screechings. The elements—
grandfather, bicycle, ditch weeds, birds,
the sun's instant—are willing together
with all of their might not to spill
and break apart.

They resist the chaos, right themselves
and continue in balance. Birds, seed-filled
weeds, grasshoppers, road dust settle
back into the silent sun.

4.

The bicycle, retaining in its skeleton
a dedication to motion and the maker
of motion, is propped against a tree
in the coming twilight calm. Grandfather,
hub and heart wavering and resuming
with falling weeds and fleeing birds,
rests in the circling frame of his sleep.
The ditch weeds and empty road,
the insects and field birds, infused
with the wheeling shadows and recoveries
of near catastrophes, are still in the revolving
light of the night. *We are all the souls
of one another,* proclaim the riding
stars, *and the soul of each moment
through which together we pass.*

The easy parting of oaks and hickories,
bays of willows, borders of pine and screens
of bamboo down to the crux, grasses, bulrushes
and reeds parting down to their fundamental
cores, the yielding of murky pond waters,
layer upon layer giving way to the touch

of the right touch, the glassy, clear
spring waters, bone and gristle alike
opening as if opening were ultimate fact,
the parting of reflection allowing passage,
and the cold, amenable skeleton of echo,
the unlatching of *marsh* becoming as easily

accessible as the unlocking of *mercy,*
as the revelation of stone splitting
perfectly with the sound of the right
sound, everything, a nubbin of corn,
a particle of power, the pose of the sky
relenting, and the sea swinging open

like the doors of a theater giving entrance
to everyone, no fences, no barriers, no blinds
to the parting of the abyss, not bolted,
not barred from the utmost offering
of the dusk, enigma itself falling away
until all may enter all and pass among them.

the
second
story

Though they will never have seen
such before, we leave special teas
in painted ceramic bowls, orange
and cherry jams, breads and linen napkins,
beside the remnants of their scattered bones.

We tie messages around green glass
bottles of wine, flasks of olives, place them
on the surface of the sea, watch them
sink slowly down to those who remain
among the rubble of their flooded shelters.
Were the current not so swift, we might
descend to deliver these gifts ourselves,
urging all to eat, to drink.

We feed their cold emptiness
with fragrances of tropical orchids,
the blossoms of magnolia and plum,
with the perfume of our prayers for solace
placed to waft inward over the ashes
of those entombed in desert caves.

Here are matches, we say to the bodies
frozen in icy passes, huddled inside ragged
animal skins, *kerosene and a lamp,*
woolen coat, metal shovel, sharpened
ax, a saddle, a horse, silver spurs.

If any should remain wanting,
yearning in their silent state, we offer
for sustenance a deeper vision of the space
where their spirits now rest, recite for them
the latitude, the longitude, the mountain
continent, the forest and prairie expanse
of their dust and decimation circling
on a vibrant globe. Nebulas and galaxies,

suns and stellar time might sooth their disquiet,
lift their souls to their rightful places.

And to all those without names, we give
more than one name: *homo habilis, homo
erectus*, fossil skeletons of rock, old
plodders, old searchers, first wielders, fierce,
steadfast clingers—and in the here and now
we are determined—the unforsaken.

I've seen this house before, simple,
clapboard, three stone steps up
to the porch, one window on each side
of the door, a hallway leading to the back.
This house appears hazy in the cool,
dim twilight of the autumn forest.
Early evening is the descending silence
of nuthatch and chickadee. Fallen leaves
cover the yard. A rake leans against
the porch post. This is a place of humans.

I've seen this house before, set against
the sharp rise of rust-colored rock spears
shadowing it in the canyon at dawn.
There's a path in the red dust,
through the dry grasses to the porch.
I smell bread here, and coffee, corn
boiling in a pot. The clink of spoon
against bowl is a singularly human sound.

I know this house. It rests on pillars
above the mucky swamp. Its roof
is covered in trumpet vines, orange-red
blossoms with wide red mouths. An anole,
green in the green shadows, jerks forward.
Mosses hang everywhere like tattered
rags of grey fringe in the tangle of cypresses
around the walls of this house. The day
is only tiny pieces of sky here. This is a human
place. Something splashes through the mud
below the porch. The dog lifts his head.
Three herons rise from their roosts.

Humans live here. Light showing
through the windows from the inside
onto the blowing snow of the plains
is human-made, human-maintained—

candle, hearth, lamp, stove. This light,
an aberration in the frozen expanse
of a black night, comes from tended
fire. Humans tend to fire.

I know this house. I hear voices inside,
syllables and variances of words, one voice,
another, unhurried, the brief murmur
of a measure of song. I'm walking up the steps.
Someone is coming to the door.

A bowl has the shape of two hands
cupped together, a shape reminiscent
of a dead turtle's shell or a hollow gourd,
a winter leaf curled and holding snow,
a human skull where the brain once lay.

This blue bowl, a fat half-belly
sitting on the table, keeps in itself,
like genes in a cell, its histories of curled
leaf and delved bone, braided reeds,
molded clay. I move my finger
along its rim in imitation of revolution,
feel the hard, clear-cut curve of its edge.
This motion of orbit in my finger
is a familiar travel, the same followed
by the moon, by a seed caught
in a whirlpool, the same circle
patterned by rain in rings on ponds,
by summer growth in the trunks
of trees. A halo is simply sunlight
shining on the rim of a bowl set free.

The character of the bowl plays
many parts—monk's bowl, beggar's
bowl, sugar bowl, fish bowl, dog's bowl,
the role of hat and a guide for barbers,
Miss Havisham's punch bowl chipped
and cracked. Kings of the past often
called for their royal bowls.

A bowl, held by both hands
up to the lips, masquerades as a cup
with milk, with tea or wine.
Whether made of brass, crystal,
hand-painted porcelain, tin, or wood—
when offered, a bowl filled with sliced

peaches, cinnamon and cream is gladly
accepted by almost everyone.

In a shell game run by a shyster,
bowls upside down can hide a coin
or nothing. Here I am, here under
the great glass bowl of the sky.

Three blackbirds tear at carrion
in a ditch, and all the light
of the stars is there too, present
in their calls, embodied in their ebony
beaks, taken into the cold wells
of their eyes, steady on the torn
strings of rotten meat in the weeds.

Starlight pierces the sea
currents and crests, touching scuds
and krill and noble sand amphipods.
It moves so steadily it is stationary
through the swill of seaweed, the fleshy
shells of purple jellyfish.

And all the light from star masses,
from constellations and clusters,
surrounds the old man walking
with his stick at night tapping the damp.
The light from those sources
exists in his beginning, interwoven
with his earliest recollections—
phrase of cradle and breath, event
of balance and reach.

Light from the stars is always
here, even with the daytime sun,
among cattle on coastal plains
and the egrets riding on their backs,
shining on the sky-side of clouds
and straight through the fog of clouds,
between white fox and white hare,
between each crystal latch to crystal
in snow. It illuminates turreted
spires and onion domes of foreign
cities, enters the stone mouths
and grimaces of saints and gargoyles,

touches the mossy roofs of weathered
barns, insect-tunneled eaves and the barbs
of owls, and all sides of each trunk
and shadow-blossom of bee trees
and willow banks, filling orchards
and aisles of almonds and plums.

The starlight comes, in union
and multiple, as weightless
as the anticipation of the barest
rain, as the slightest suggestion
of a familiar voice sounding
in the distance. It is as common,
as fulsome as the air of a mellow
time with no wind. The light
of the stars encompasses everything,
even until and beyond the final cold
passing of the last cinder-bone
and minim of the vanished earth.

makes more silver the silver
buckle on the rapist's belt, makes
more august the silver nailheads
in the doorpost, subsumes

all rain-held silver as it falls.
This history enables long blades

of blowing grasses to cut cleanly
and precisely through the darkness like old
definitions of sun forged and honed.

It elaborates on the belly and teeth

of the shortfin mako sweeping
into its mouth the brilliance
of the herring's gleaming body,

further elucidates the white ribbons
of the rabbit's blood spilled among
mountain boulders where the bobcat
feeds. It distinguishes the yellow

eyes of the jackal, the slitted eyes
of the hyena, the closed eyes

of the stone wall, the lidless,
the frozen eyes of opals and winter
ponds. The long history of starlight

at night possesses, like any song,
like any death, dependable borders
across which one might pass
to disappear, pass to emerge,

secures, like a locked room, a radius
where sworn declarations in light
hover in circles like men conspiring,

encompasses, like a cave, an emptiness
where the blind, the albino, the luminous

spiral and the luminous wheel

and the bald heads of destroying
angels signal and burn, keeps,
like a cold lantern inside its closed

glass space, the real possibility
of error, the actual right to awaken.

All of us urged them to rise up
out of the earth and go on a moonless
midnight, to go by all means. We told
them it was essential for their lacking
souls. We said you'll encounter
in that wide open sky a black blacker
than the one blindness you know, a black
so deep it throbs like the root passion
in your own gut, trembles like desert
rock beneath the hooves of frightened
horses, rings throughout with the brilliant
quantum edges of distance.

We said you'll witness there the churning
hive of your origins, the holy implements
of transfiguration, and the tomes
of ancient kin, the maps of emboldened
navigators who, like you, moved
in journeys through darkness.

We instructed. We preached.
We explained and cajoled. But how
could they go so far into such manifold
and incantatory spheres? those little
naked mole rats in their tunnel networks
below the earth? How could they emerge
to travel so, with only stumpy limbs
for legs, with their dirt-covered digging
fangs protruding awkwardly like tusks,
with neither coats nor capes to guard
their wrinkled bare bodies from
the chill night air? And how could
they see to go with nothing but shallow
skin-covered sockets for eyes, with no
lantern to fill with fire, with no word
for a boundless heavenly hallow, with no

word for beyond–the–mole–rat–self,
with no known void to fill with vision?

With no sign or query or hunger
for the heart-sensed starlights
of the *forever* missing from their faithful
old souls, how could they rise
into what they could never imagine?

We turned away from them then
and departed, afraid.

As they talked and mingled together,
the earth, the size of an orange, floated
among them through the room, slowly
turning on its axis with a not unpleasant
hum, vibrating low like the strum
of bass strings. It seemed wrapped
in silk by its clouds.

And it traveled in its orbit across
the open plains, over cornfields, keeping
pace with the train, along rushes
and scrub willows lining the creek beds.
Cattle in the fields never raised
their heads. Following the empty
tracks at night, it was a pure white
pebble speeding through the black
against the dimmer stars.

No one on board the ship
in the thundering storm noticed
the earth dawning out of the horizon,
shining like a nugget of diamond
with sea rain and salt. And in the spotlight
at the Cirque du Soleil, it was merely
one of nine balls circling the juggler's
head. Drums rolled. Cymbals rang.
Nothing faltered, not globes, not performer.
How its polar ice caps gleamed blue!
The audience applauded politely.

If it had been observed as itself,
it might have been seen fitting perfectly
in the hand of Christ, on the Buddha's
lap, cradled like a pearl in a shell,
cherished like a spark of mouse

in the night of a coyote's eye, rich
and wild with reverence.

The size of a crow's head, it was
that distinct against the snow as it flew
on its path, that bright through the fog,
that accurate in its courses, that brilliant
in its spheres.

Last night in parted clouds,
      we couldn't distinguish the stars falling

    from the snow falling—both cold, deadly,
        and inviting, both distant
    and magnetic in their indefinite

        places, both erudite in silence,
both traveling by sleep, both against black,

      both against white, against the trickery
          of the eye, against revelation,
      against immortality,

    both boneless, as naked as light, neither

    beckoning, neither denying, both ancients
        broken and unchronicled,

      both out of the pit
    into the instant and back, both cracking
      the continuum,
            rushing down
    in multitudes toward the earth
as if it were the Holy Grail, the grave,

    both in diamonds, both in spades, all aces—
      the way things were for awhile last night.

A monk at night, hooded and robed
in black, disappears into the side door
of a monastery.

Or is it a shadow of wind vanishing
into a cave in a hillside that seems
in the dark to be a monastery built
like a hillside with bell towers and spires?

A starry hill is robed like a monastery
in chants and processions, hooded by night
like a bell tower at prayer. The wind moves
with a penance across the night sky
ringing like a monastery vanishing
into the cave of its own ceremonies.

A monk emerges backward from penance
into the world as if out of the crease
of the night's horizon black as the mouth
of a cave or a bell and its shadow.
There is definitely motion
and the transformation of confusion.

Carrying rake and shovel, a monk
disappears at vespers through a simple
wooden door in the wall of a monastery
and enters the evening star.

The wind rises now, blows back
my hood, opens my robe like a doorway
to night. The hillside of stars is entering
with its monastery of shadows.
I am the heaven of auguries.

They collected them one by one
like seed–size pearls and put them
in their black velvet bags, gathered
them like small marbles of amethyst
and alabaster, plucked them
like white cherries from a tree.

They placed all of them carefully
in their velvet bags scarcely filled.
And they were patient, gathering
them slowly all their lives, some
like berries of glass, like the slighter
fruit of mistletoe, some appearing
like tiny flames flashing on sunless
river bottoms or shining like quick silver
schools of fish in the deep. A few
were as cold and black and enigmatic
as skull sockets where eyes should be.

When the end came, they crawled
into their black velvet sacks themselves,
pulled the drawstrings tight over
their heads, looked around and above
in the speckled dark and more than once
toward the east, then assembled
their instruments and resumed the study
of their everlasting treasures —Sirius,
Polaris, Arcturus, Capella, Vega,
Andromeda, Cygnus X, guides,
messengers, hope.

the
third
story

It takes practice to be able to see the formless
suggestion of what is never seen, as, just
beyond the farthest prairie horizon that the eyes
can define, the fragment of a nonexistent
motion might be missing its blind
spirit on horseback unnoticed.

So faint, so slight to the vision,
much less detectable than the moon
on a cloudy, moonless night—maybe
there is no nonessence faltering around
the shape of the sweet yellow flag,
as I once believed, a quivering lack
so false it can't bear the weight of a name.

Standing beside the churling whitecaps
at the canyon rim of a descending sea,
someone denies proposing the state
of a dead white woman rising with the surf
to sing in silence of her own absence.
And in the skyward dissolution of fog
disappearing in shades above the field
of mountain snow, there is nothing
implying its non-presence or possibility,
no purpose of ice refusing to remark on itself.

Can it be real, a fact so illusory
among the parsnip and minty skullcap
of the wetlands that it has not as yet
even hinted at its own unreality?

How shall I speak in truth of the momentary,
starry realm spreading forever as a lie
unwitnessed inside the black call
of the crow at dusk?

This blatancy is too subtle: the freedom
to say *my unbound voice struggling
against its bars and chains.*

Outside the realm of breath and bone,
of vision with eyes, outside a sentient
vein of any kind, outside the tangible
or any of those ways we ordinarily tell
ourselves of presence, there may be a place
where one could be fire, for instance,
not a body lit by the light of fire,
not a body hearing the humming furnace
of fire or watching the orange, ash-
rimmed coals of fire fading, but a place
where one might be the fire itself,
if *be* is the right word for such a state,
if *state* has definition in such a realm.

Perhaps in this place one might,
if one wished, be merely motion—not
the wind or plains of grasses swathed
by wind, not a canyon wren in flight
passing a cliff edge, gliding straight out
over the echoing blue gorge below, not
the rise and hush of a river at the height
of spring, be none of these but the motion
alone of each, without weight or force,
without shadow, without domain.

One might exist (or some similar
word for being) not as soil or rock
or sea cave, not as any blossom
or animal blustering of the earth
but as its orbit, and not the path itself
but the equation the earth creates against
the starry background of its passages,
exist as the sublime math of the earth
in its revolution, not numbers
or symbols on paper, but the soaring
right of the math, that entity, if *entity*
is correct in these circumstances,

45

if *circumstance* exists in this place,
if *place* be a concept of equation.

Three horses stand together in the chill
autumn dusk. The lowered heads
of the bay and her sister are touching,
the silver fog of their breaths meeting.
The third, a pinto, stands perpendicular
to the others, faces the haunch of the bay.
Maybe in this place I could be the design
these horses make in relation to one another
against the sky, be the sort of beautiful
purity a design like that can make,
if that is what I am, if *I am* is anyone.
It could be fun in a place like that.
Or something even better.

Knock, and it shall be opened . . . MATTHEW 7:7

Sometimes it's like a ticking,
like the ticking metal makes as it cools,
or the random clicking the rafters make
as the house shifts in the wind.

The same insistence is always present,
whether its sound is sharp like a ring rapping
against glass or like one loose shingle
flapping directly overhead.

It can clatter rapidly, like teeth
clicking from cold, like bones tossed
for a prophecy, like stones rolled
by a current, rattling together unseen
over the river bottom. It pauses,
as if to reconsider, then resumes,
like the tapping of an old man's foot
as he rocks through a summer dusk,
sporadic as the hammering of a woodpecker
in a hardwood forest, first far, then near.

It is reverberant in the tocking sounds
of hail striking rocky ground, the same
sound heard in the ritual languages
of high desert peoples.

It maintains a constancy like the clacking
wheels of a train on the tracks passing
through the countryside or like the rhythmic
catching of wheels in a clock passing
through time as if it were a landscape.

Something abroad is knocking.
Something pervasive, resolved, unknown,
seeks entrance. Imagine unlatching
the gate. Envision what may pass
through among us. Pretend to answer.

There are faces everywhere outside
the fence. I see them deep in the grasses,
staring, grimacing, multi-eyed, bald,
some earless, some with thin and crooked
snouts, some with open mouths, some
with no mouths at all, an audience,
a crowd in the field outside the fence.

All are agile, adaptable among
the tall grasses. If a shadow should pass
over them or if the sweet red fennel
should bend slightly in a wind and brush
against them, they vanish instantly
into the cruder structures of their features,
the stalk-and-stem outline of their basic state,
the original leaf-and-seed version of themselves.

Some faces blink, look away, look back.
What is it they see? Some sink and sleep
and never wake. What vision is their
nightmare? There is a face clear and stark
in the flat rock of the cliff above the creek.
Viewed from upside down, however,
it disappears, retreating into the blank
and enduring stone soul of itself. We might
envy the essence of such a transformation.

There are winter faces in snow patches
and open black earth on the northern
hillsides, and narrow faces lengthening
across the field as evening advances, night
faces fidgeting at the shadow edges
of the streetlight. There's a face in the wooden
box in the corner of the church, a face
in the stirred water of the baptismal font,
a forlorn and wistful face in the dripped

wax pooled at the candle's base. It fattens,
it closes its eyes, it grows cold.

We see by being seen. We are never
alone where we are. There are faces
even the blind can't see.

a mystic in the garden mistakes
lizards for ghosts and extrapolates
on same

One slight shiver and flutter of blue
morning glory, a leaf tip resonating
with no wind, a switch, a quick scritch
(was it?) in the dry thatches beneath the ivy,
a shadow left shaking—ghosts are
everywhere in this garden, each a cause
sensed but never seen among the heavy
vines of wisteria, the blossoms of purple
aster and white phlox along the paths.

They are a brief turn sensed just once,
like the supposed click of a key heard
in a foreign realm and never heard again,
like the last strum of strings remembered
after the player has gone. They are a slit
of night in daytime, fitting exactly the mossy
cracks in the stone wall, disappearing
down those tunnels to whatever hell
or heaven exists for them there.

What is sensed of these ghosts
is only the moment witnessed just after
their vanishing. Where they were
is all that they are.

They may have eyes the color
of mirrors that stare with the steadiness
of glass. They may have porous bodies
like ponds in rain, like the diaphanous
wings of dragonflies in sun. They may have
tails indistinguishable from the skeletal
blades of dead grasses, move on feet
as quiet and precise as cobwebs.

Surely within the insubstantial
bone marrow of these ghosts live
all the ghosts of themselves existing
in their past manifestations of absence,
the hauntings and sleights of their
ancestral gardens. This is the way
ghosts achieve immortality.

And certainly they must worship
in silence an eternally vanishing god,
almost witnessed, almost possessed,
created naturally in the likeness
of themselves. A god of ghosts
who is not a ghost, after all, would be
a very strange thing.

The ghosts of this garden are like
the emptiness of pods and husks
under midnight snow when the moon
has passed, like the pause following
the clank and lock of the gate
at dusk, like the inevitable in motion
beyond the cosmic horizon. Strange,
what void these ghosts would leave
should the garden be ever without them.

The landscape in this country is entirely
bare and blank, undistinguished
by any feature, except for a stitch
of swallows appearing and disappearing

above the sky-smooth lake, in and out
through the portals invented by their own
journeys. Here alone is absence, except
for many tiny punctures in the overall,

seeming like the prints of thorny grass
crickets, the pinpoint instincts of gripping
lizard toes, the stinging bristles of musk
thistle and the lesser spikes of lattice

spider. This is a dull, unbroken scape,
except for a pinnacle, a balustrade of forest,
except for a rip of hound yelping and then
another, and the jagged red slash

of a rooster's occasional "chicchirichi,"
except for a multitude of cracks in the oblivion
through which appear many eyes, yellow
of black cat on a tile roof, pierce of preying

gull, two glassy prongs of woodland
snail, old man in grey cap with cigarette.
This country is still and void, except
for a funnel of attention from which

emerges an imagination lacking all
countenance until it begins together
with *a skitter of lizard nails, an old man
flicking ash, a two-pronged snail*

and its glistening swill, a vista of gull's eye
at prey, the play of chicchirichi, a lake of sky
opened by swallow doorways to form
the creation of its own reality.

When lying beneath a ponderosa
pine, looking up through layers
of branches, mazes of leaf-spikes
and cones—contemplation grows
receptive to complexity,
the pleasant temptation of pine-
scented tangle. Sky as proposition
is willingly divided and spliced
into a thesis of weaves and hallows.

Name them something else
if you wish, but needled shadow
and substance are, in this hour,
an architecture of philosophy.

And a rising wind, called "a rough
and bawdy wind" by a rough and bawdy
voice, is that wind and that voice
transformed. The structure of words
sways and bends in the blow.

Looking away into the clear sky,
expectation shifts. Vision becomes
a welcome to guests of crows in new
dimensions who themselves become
not only depth and horizon in a circus
of wings but old vision's startling visitors.

Not soul alone, but soul consumed
by a single bee descending into the center
of a purple mountain lily is soul
to a soul suckled in sleep.

Earth and human together
form a unique being. A brief era
of immortality is lent to each
by the other. Move momentarily

now—with hovering granite cliff,
with sun-stripe flick of perhaps
vagrant shrew, with raised tack
of mighty larkspur—into this company.

Spirits are rising even now
out of the spines of sleeping hyena,
camel, steppe fox, golden jackal,

emanating from the points of gizzard
shad, bonefish, bee fly, stream creeper,
shades and the sovereignty of shades,

out of the breasts of dormant pika
and singing vole and up through the deep
from musk turtle and crayfish buried

in a pond-bottom mud like the most definite
of invisible intentions, images coming through
the shards and errors of storms and droughts,

beyond mangrove swamps, over
the rims of rolling taiga tides and snow
fields, the patterns of city sparrow,

ribbon seal, porpoise and pigeon emerging
from all night and farther back, spirits,
apprehensions of scab worm and lug

worm, blue pitta and biting louse,
singular, on their own, the idea of lantern bug,
corncrake, nut clam and great piddock,

infant and crone, by heaven, by earth,
rain or wind, not merely phantom or specter,
but the defining crux of dead-leaf

cricket, bushbuck, springbok,
implication of prawn and spider shell,
force of rufous-handed howler, reef

heron and bush pig appearing in essence
like the first stars of their own bones,
finfoot, trumpeter, lily-trotter, diamond

and jesting, as emblematic as the breath
of caves, as assertive as a cusp or crescent
of stone against sky, and where

they will arrive, there a single word,
surpassing and unequivocal, will be arriving
simultaneously to enfold them.

the
fourth
story

The leg of one is hooked around
and forcing the knee of the other,
who is flipped, knocked suddenly
to the ground, a roll and thrust
to upright, quick turn, the full nelson,
hands pressing hard behind the neck.

Both struggle, sweaty, grimacing
and cursing. They spit with the effort,
snort and groan from their bellies
like hogs, red-faced, stamping. Dust
rises from the old boards. One heaves
and lifts the other on her back, off
her feet, breaks the hold, flips face
to face. Clinging body to body,
they fight to choke each other at the ribs,
encircling arms squeezing tight.

The rickety nightstand rocks.
The lamp dims, sways, tumbles,
snaps the connection. The foot
of one fights the ankle of the other,
maneuvering for position. Bare
soles and heels squeak on the waxed
wood. They fall to the floor, dragging
each other down. Nightgowns tangle
and rip, showing frayed cotton knickers.
A sleeve tears, a bodice slips as they claw
and scramble, one on top straddling,
then beneath, pressed and held to the floor.

The clock goes black. Atomic structure
falters. Teeth are deep in a shoulder.
A furious cry. There's an odor here
of salt, of ozone, of chlorine, a sound
like ocean blowing and hissing, thudding

against the shore, energy of the ruthless,
power of the unrelenting.

The steam, the streaking mucous and slick
rancid reekings of each perspiring body
are assumed by the other, the harsh
gut breath. Were they to cease, to part,
were they to surrender or subdue, neither
would have a name, no spine of hell,
no hard grasp of heaven.

Out the door, bursting hinge
and lock, into the rain and storm—
a lightning bolt shows blue fire
on a boulder—they lurch down
the hillside pummeling each other,
over the rocks and assailing thorns,
through mud and rivulets, a melee
of knuckle and nail, scrambling
and flailing, latched together
forever—like moon and engine,
like fire and bell, like wren
and silence—for their own sakes.

He must measure the average
length of the fangs and each claw
unsheathed, calculate the reach
of the forelimbs, the maximum
expanse of the leap.

By sleeping on the grasses
of their abandoned beds, he can become
accustomed to the smothering odors
of their fur and hide, learn to anticipate
the sudden dizzying musk of their resonant
bodies and thereby hope to maintain
equilibrium in their presence.

The clever feint and dodge, the pistol
loaded with blanks, the report of the whip
snapped in midair will often stay
a treachery. Fire of candle or small torch
thrust quickly forward by surprise
may momentarily keep desertion at bay.
Not one must be damaged.

He attends to the plaint of their roarings—
how the sound imitates in possibility
the breadth of the starry savannah,
in certainty the thunderous sky
of wildebeests in stampede. He must read
and absorb the entire vocal range
of their rages and victories, the lesser
growls and spittings of their lovemaking.

Here are the bones, the blackened blood
left from their feedings. All of them
eat flesh and lick the leavings.

Perhaps they will sit still on their small
stools and wait, watching him. Perhaps

they will saunter snarling in a line
around the ring and stop to rise reluctantly
on their hind legs before him, meet
his eyes, imitate prayer.

If the nuance of the fake charge
is mastered, if the dance of the tail
is interpreted, if the prophecy of pant
and crouch is forsworn, then the time
may arrive when pity will appear among them
and the door of the cage open, and he will
step out, released and resurrected.

One of the most common whistlers,
found everywhere on earth,
is the wind, whistling with the furl
and strafe of cattail marshes
in autumn or roughly around
the naked stone nymphs of formal
gardens, rasping across desert sands,
high-pitched and hardy in northern
blizzards above icy ocean plains,
or sounding the soft moan
of a spring night in easy sleep.

Some people claim stars belong
in this classification too, because stars,
comets and even the moon, have often
been heard all together whistling
in their multitudes of clear glass
tones late on solitary winter nights.

The whistling of the black-bellied
whistling ducks in their tree-top perches
is shrill in its refrains, while the Arctic
tundra actually becomes quite musical
with the whistlings of the whistling
swans in summer. Humpback whales
whistle underwater, a singular feat.
Some creatures whistle in warning,
as the hoary marmot and the woodchuck do;
some whistle in pain; some with relief.
Some whistle through their fingers
for fun, or through a blade of grass,
or through wood or wax contrivances
fashioned solely for this purpose.

Mephistopheles, surely a member
of this genus, whistled in agony,
a high screeching signal of ruin

as he rolled and writhed across the heavens,
defeated and banished, falling forever.
Such a piteously shrieking sound
he made disappearing like the whistle
of a train vanishing across a prairie.

Once at night I heard the low
beseeching whistle of someone
calling to me from a secret place,
calling to me to come, sounding
like the longing of a night bird
beseeching his lover to come
to his secret place.

I don't know anything about god
whistling, unless god is the wind,
unless god is the black-bellied duck
whistling high in a tree, or the hoary
marmot alarmed, or a boy for fun
blowing on a blade of grass held
between his hands, or a lover calling,
invisible and loved, unless god
is the will to whistle, ancient,
abundant, perfectly expressive
in all its forms, a will that wills to be
every manifestation of its own will.

If god was a cow, I could lead him
by a rope through a ring in his nose,
hang a bell around his neck, always
hear him wherever he was, even alone
in the open night. I could feed him
and fatten him. I could take him to clover
and fields of new grasses, put hay
on the snow for him in winter. I could
walk him to shelter out of hailstones
and thunderstorms, through the smoke
of summer fires, past trailing wolves, free him
from thorny bramble and cactus patches.

If god was a cow, I could slaughter him.
I could bludgeon him in the head
between the eyes with a hammer,
crack his skull, see his brains seeping.
I could watch his legs crumple under him
as he sank to the ground. I could feel
in the shake of the earth, and remember,
the weight of him as he fell.

I could eat him, drain his blood,
cook his blood and spoon it in
like soup. I could roast him, savor
his flanks and ribs and simmering
fat, absorb his fragrances, the perfumes
of his waft and smoke. I could skin him
and tan his hide and fashion his hide
and wear his hide as shoes, as hat,
as weskit, be covered by the pelt
of god, walk inside of god.

I could say, "I know you, god.
It was I who named you *cow*.
I have kept you, prepared you,
honored you, watched over you.

I have borne witness to you. After all,
I butchered you with care and skill.
I cut you open to the core. I uncovered
your parts. I touched all of your parts,
your secret parts. I have tasted you,
chewed you up, swallowed you,
sucked your bones and spit them out,
bleached your empty skull and hung it
high on my wall. I have wanted
you. I have needed you. You
have become and forsaken me.
In this we must both be satisfied."

If he chooses, his voice can come
directly from a sycamore in the voice
of the sycamore,
               for instance, the words
seeming to rise right out of the branches
and broad, ovate leaves, intoning
like autumn in its hanging balls of nutlet
seeds.

       By him, the damp summer grasses
in their limber statement ask the question
he poses.
           The fat cattails in their statuary
marsh
        give his response. Rain striking
the lake delivers his soliloquy in its periodic
constancy. This is the soliloquy he recites
as the speech of falling rain.

            He cries
as the coyote wailing with his mother's
grief. He bemoans as an evening shadow
suffering his brother's passing.
             As himself,
he addresses himself as the wind,
its voice his voice in stone narrative
along the sheer edge
             of the bluff where
they appear momentarily together
in this act.

    When he discourses
as the lead glass vase of yellow tulips
on the sill, some might wonder who
directs this conversation.
            He talks

with himself, so the street lamp and its circle
of light always tell him.

                    Does he speak as death
with dry leaves vanishing
                    in an open fire?
Or are the burning tongues of dry leaves
the oratory of fiery life
                    he translates?
Or does the language of fire illuminate
death vanishing
                    like dry leaves
in translation?

                    Can't you hear the abyss
speaking now as the soul
                    of the wooden
puppet he holds on his lap
                    and answers,
moving its mouth, whispering in its ear?

Masked and tooled, I begin
moving through the rock
corridors of these underground
waters, through the black

channels and caves of these rivers
existing far beneath the white
expanse of forests and roofs
and fields so open to the sky,

so still within the spatial
silence of snow. I imagine
moving deliberately in the night
beneath this winter landscape,

pausing and proceeding, mapping
the many passageways carved
and flooded by the rising seas
of past retreating glaciers

and ancient mountains of ice,
the welling of freshwater springs.
As I inch along the stone
hallways, marking the network

of their patterns, the complex
flow of their tidal and rainfall
currents, I imagine I am sitting
in this chair beside this window

watching the pale grey edge
of the horizon slowly blur
with snow and vanish. I can see
that the universe of winter snow

is merely light lit from within,
illumination suffused and expanding
in all dimensions. I recognize
myself residing within the equation

of this configuration. I close my eyes
and rest there. The torch I carry
in these black river tunnels, mazed
like catacombs, sputters inside its glass.

I falter. It re-ignites. I remember
and resume. Through time and time
again, without stars or sun, among
the cilia of tiny albino creatures,

the swirl of transparent fish,
the fragile weave of their skeletons
more imagined than witnessed,
among the staring blindness

of the primordial and the unidentified,
I adhere to the turns and necessities
of my direction. In the chair beside
this window, I hold my wrappings close,

will my way along these submerged
galleries, aim for the juncture
where all rivers flowing from all
dimensions converge. I imagine

I will be indivisible—so the solid
night of rivers underground,
so the light of winter, so fact
and anti-fact—in the confluence
of that creation.

Coming, cursing, with his stick raised,
he routs the geese from the garden,
the chickens from the kitchen, the phantom
from the marsh, the alleyway. Swinging
and swishing, he thrashes severely
the fearsome nothing behind the door.

He uses the stick in April to draw
furrows, to prod, to make spaces
in the plowed earth where he plants
pieces of potato, seeds of carrots,
corn, marigold.

In the forest, he flips over a stone
with his stick, beneath which we find
eleven pill bugs, one white spider, a hard,
glistening spot of land snail. With the tip
of the stick, he discovers and touches
lightly the fleshy stem of the wild celery,
the pungent rootstock of the sweet flag.

He measures the depth of the pool,
lowering the stick straight down
to the bottom where the mud
salamander settles and the brown clam
lies. Almost submerged entirely,
it's nearly lost in the process.

He holds it to his eye in the field.
He sights along its length to find true
north, to fix our location. With his stick
he can strike the cross of the coordinates
exactly. He can write directions
in soft soil or sands.

At night he holds it high as it points
to Rigel, Capella, the Great Galaxy
in Andromeda. He circles it above
his head to trace the diurnal motion
of the stars around Polaris.

Later, he hobbles a little. He leans
on his stick. It makes his way home.

the
fifth
story

This is about no rain in particular,
just any rain, rain sounding on the roof,
any roof, slate or wood, tin or clay
or thatch, any rain among any trees,
rain in soft, soundless accumulation,
gathering rather than falling on the fir
of juniper and cedar, on a lace-community
of cobwebs, rain clicking off the rigid
leaves of oaks or magnolias, any kind
of rain, cold and smelling of ice or rising
again as steam off hot pavements
or stilling dust on country roads in August.
This is about rain as rain possessing
only the attributes of any rain in general.

And this is about night, any night
coming in its same immeasurably gradual
way, fulfilling expectations in its old
manner, creating heavens for lovers
and thieves, taking into itself the scarlet
of the scarlet sumac, the blue of the blue
vervain, no specific night, not a night
of birth or death, not the night forever
beyond the frightening side of the moon,
not the night always meeting itself
at the bottom of the sea, any sea, warm
and tropical or starless and stormy, night
meeting night beneath Arctic ice.
This attends to all nights but no night.

And this is about wind by itself,
not winter wind in particular lifting
the lightest snow off the mountaintop
into the thinnest air, not wind through
city streets, pushing people sideways,
rolling ash cans banging down the block,
not a prairie wind holding hawks suspended

mid-sky, not wind as straining sails
or as curtains on a spring evening, casually
in and back over the bed, not wind
as brother or wind as bully, not a lowing
wind, not a high howling wind. This is
about wind solely as pure wind in itself,
without moment, without witness.

Therefore this night tonight—
a midnight of late autumn winds shaking
the poplars and aspens by the fence, slamming
doors, rattling the porch swing, whipping
thundering black rains in gusts across
the hillsides, in batteries against the windows
as we lie together listening in the dark, our own
particular fingers touching—can never
be a subject of this specific conversation.

1.

The ear, being boneless and almost always
exposed, except in icy, windy weather,
possesses a rather charming vulnerability,
an innocent faith in the purpose of its presence.
Never changing its strange expression,
it waits patiently, a pure *waiting* in the flesh,
to apprehend all sounds coming its way,
the creaks and whines, the bangs and chirps
of the universe roiling and bubbling.

2.

The lobe of the ear is especially exquisite,
soft as a bud of rosebay, even softer,
being warm as well and smooth
as a moonstone. I once knew a woman
whose cat sucked the lobe of her ear
like a nipple, purring and humming
in a trance of nuzzling.

Lovers often seek the earlobe this way too.
And all those curves and crevices
and hidden places of the ear are tempting
to the exploring tongue of a lover probing
and searching as if believing there were god–
inspired secrets, visions to be discovered
in the darkness of those bewildering ways.

Each ear is unique in its rare geography,
its particular hollows and furrows different
from any other, the rim rounded like an aspiring
hillock. The lover's tongue can always
recognize the ear it possesses, the delved
and canyoned land it has traveled.

3.

There is a certain tuck in the outer ear,
a small fold, the vestige of a remote ancestor,
an ancient ancestor perhaps fanged
and clawed, nomadic and hard, an ancestor
who might sever our spines, puncture
our hearts, were we to meet each other today.
Put your finger on that fold. Touch
that old, old vanished kin, the dim
and perished who bore, the living ghost
you own but may never remember.

4.

There was a warrior who made a necklace
of the ears of his victims and wore it
daily with honor. Peter took his sword
and struck off the right ear of Malchus
in the Garden of Gethsemane. Researchers
recently grew a human ear on the back
of a mouse. Some babies have been born
with ears closed tight like fists, the flesh
curled into itself, as if the sounds
of the universe were too horrid to bear.
Elegant or protruding, loved or not,
the ear can be a comical feature. Clowns
wearing large rubber ears always
get laughs. The ear has its own stories,
its own myths. Listen.

He holds the flute to his mouth,
though all of his fingers are gone,
a portion of his face and one ear
broken away.

His head is slightly cocked,
his lips pursed, his pose casual,
as if he didn't notice the tight
leaves of grey lichen growing
up his legs undisturbed, the greener
mosses in deeper, damper places,
the black bee resting near
the crack in his forehead.

His contemplative eyes,
where his eyes have vanished,
suggest he is listening to an inner
song before the song arrives.

He is unclothed, except for the skin
of a wildcat draped over one shoulder,
its boneless paws, its hollow head
hanging, seeming accustomed, evidently
from the first, to diminishment
and missing parts.

With a prophecy that hardly
matters, the shadow of the camphor
tree in bloom, beside which he stands,
spreads across his face and torso
through the day, passes him by
to touch and linger on the ledge
above the lake.

There is a definite music here
with him, though we remain

perplexed as to the harmonies
it employs, the odd key in which
it is composed, what breath it is
that sounds it.

The Villa Serbelloni
Bellagio, Italy

"Throughout the evening the purpling
    yellow signatures of the sky appear
        and disappear as ragged
changelings
    between the flittering leaves
  of the lombardy hedges.
        Then begins the mad tittering

of mad frogs lumpy as gold
      nuggets in the glinting gold light
  of sun through pond waters.

All around stand, unmoving,
    many one-legged beings—cadres
      of cattails, a hollow cottonwood,

windfall willow of willow, blue stilt
  of heron resting in reedy brush.

The sparks of the shad flies,
        orbiting themselves in the slant
   light, are self-replicating
  testaments to the orbiting starry
spheres of the night, their own begotten

     children. Single and virgin,
   the slender gypsum moon comes
      glancing either right

or left. As a pale orb weaver plucks
  his nuptial cadenza,
     the glimmering strands
         of the web tremble
a flourish like a small and hopeful
  aria of fire,"

   so sing at once in the attentive hall
    the concert's
      six-part voices.

A coyoteevening cries with orange
and scarlet howls, then thrice
circles itself before settling into sleep.

The wingleaves of freed poplar birds
never lift to circumnavigate the seas;
nevertheless they disappear periodically,
make untraceable journeys alone
and return to themselves every spring.

Only a cactuswolf can lick and smooth
the thorns of another cactuswolf
without sustaining multiple injuries
to the tongue. Taming the cactuswolf,
which often implies transplanting cur,
bitch and sire, involves days of harsh
sun, much finesse and patience,
and unique equipment beyond rope,
muzzle, shovel and leather gloves.

The crowberry and the batberry,
cultivated exclusively in large
light-controlled cages, are pure
and alluring. Their fat bodies hang
or perch in clusters from their summer
vines. They are especially prized
for the floating sky-visions induced
by both blackbatberry wine
and crowberry cobbler.

Fernghosts of lost rainforests
often haunt the conservatories
of the wealthy, drifting down the aisles,
passing through the latticework
to chill, with their icy fingerfronds
and invisible snow-like spores,
guests, lovers and gardeners alike.

The Sabbathrose never blooms;
for the Sabbath, as we know, is strictly
a day of rest. The Sabbathrose
is, therefore, self-contradictory
and simply the fabrication
of a heathen imagination.

These interdisciplinary studies
are being assembled by those venerated
experts responsible for discovering
and translating heretofore lost
beetlescrolls, sanddunedocuments,
the ritual anthems of tumbleweedchoirs
and the webscriptures of orchard spiders.

from a simple vanilla vortex
come voices of the faithful

1.

Here is sweet vanilla grass
for flavoring fine-cut tobacco,
for scenting the houses of the poor,
for strengthening the brain, for filling
bed pillows to induce lucid, mellow
sleep and dreams of a mild-tempered god.

2.

No one has ever been murdered
on forest trails among trees having
bark that smells of vanilla, not even
inside the last winter midnight
of the new moon.

3.

To cure rude disposition and *mal de tete*
of summer, take ice cold oranges
with vanilla ice cream at sunset

4.

"Four-and-twenty vanilla birds
baked in a pie," was recited long before
there were kings or queens, pastries
or ovens, eons before there were
numbers or melodies, even before
the first knife executed the first
opening cut of the crust and the release
of the beginning began in wild flurries
flying forth across the realm.

5.

Ritual Chants from the Insane advise:
Choose for sacrament the golden vanilla
wafer (wafer of the divine), in contrast
to the burnt-sugar and anise biscuit
(black biscuit of mad minions).

6.

Remember, it is into the vortex
of the white orchid of *V. planiforia*
(from which comes the vanilla bean
and its sensual oils), it is upon the soft
fluted lips of that flower and into the deep
funnel of its elaborate spread that the truly
devout servant must place ears, mouth,
tongue, fingers, so as to receive fully
into the vortex of the soul all messages
of transcendence inherent to that hallowed space.

Drink from this circle of night right here,
blind and sudden with currents and waves
like the wellside of the moon.

Put your mouth here where I'm showing you,
against this darkness as full of the taste
of sky as snow water caught early
in clean cave rock.

Easy between your lips again and again,
roll this slight berry possessing
the texture of violet at the root,
having the nature of a solid grain
of clear, flowing river.

Swallow at this narrow crevassing
shadow of faint salt whose ending can never
be savored or known. Tongue this tight,
gathered petal and that other small winding
of rose too, with its glassy sap.

Lick here, round and round this warm
nub, a taste a little like butter and sea,
a little like liquid sun left
on dense green mosses after dusk.

Close your eyes, and where I'm placing
your finger, here at this single flume,
like a funnel of iris leaf lithe
and rolled at the stem, suck
morning.

At this swelling, from this soft
cistern, from this heated damp like wet
day on summer grasses, drink first.

Then answer me.

Monet painted his wife dressed in white
standing on a rise against the summer
sky, holding a white parasol. Madama
Butterfly's maidens, wending up the hillside
to her wedding, carried small parasols
to shade their faces. And haughty Miss Rosie,
on her way to the warden to free her man,
rested her umbrella casually on her shoulder.

I once saw tap dancers in yellow
slickers twirling their black umbrellas
around and around before them
as they clicked and clacked across the stage.

Centuries ago a Princess of Ethiopia,
wearing a robe of apple-green satin,
rode beneath one, its gold tassels
swaying and flashing with sun
like strings of fire around her head
as the people watched her majesty pass.
Like the moon, like music, like anger,
an umbrella is an event in any design
through which it moves.

Somewhere on earth right now,
a large-bosomed clown finally opens
her wobbly parasol of bare stick
ribs, ribs as bare as the skeleton
of a fish an alley cat has left,
lifts it high and promenades
proudly around the circus ring,
a scattered parade of clowns
marching out of step behind her.

Like rolling pins and brooms,
umbrellas have often been used
effectively by women as weapons.

Some are made of silk, some of oiled
leather or skin, some of feathers.
Sun umbrellas with bamboo staves
are of translucent colored paper painted
with plum or cherry blossoms, a cricket
perched on a stem, three geese in flight
before the full moon. Maybe the very first
was a leaf taken from an umbrella tree,
a subtle suggestion offered by god.

Stories as shelter, like umbrellas,
open and expand and they close
and fold away.

I.

We watched each closely, strolling
and stopping from one to the next.
We saw a woman with a pearl-fringed
parasol standing in the sun on an arching
bridge, and a panther, small within the equatorial
forests, lurking alone in the wild eyes
of his own moonless night.

In the hall where we were, a warrior
with grey and purple face held a dripping
sword in one hand, the severed head
of his enemy in the other. Wind and dust
were swirling in from the east.

Once we were lost in an expanding
caucus of spring grasses, red poppies
and violet asters. Once a feathered
goddess of war, sneering and posturing,
showed her sharpened teeth and fat
tongue. Once, nearly falling off, a clown
rode before us on a long-legged rooster.

We stared, five gold and black-pearl fish
in a pond of lilies, the glistening metal
svelte of their bodies in the still water.

II.

We were of them all momentarily until
we left the place, wondering after the living
presence manifest in the dead dimensions
of each event with its scope of light.

What nature compelled the signal blue
of the violet asters? What engaging force
defined the character of the word
lurking in the panther's moon-brilliant

green eyes, the unique vision seen
within the blind eyes of the severed
head held aloft in the wind by its hair?

How were we to distinquish
the red life in the field poppies
from the red life in the spilled blood
dripping on the ground from the red
life of *red* and its living color from
the invisible red life implicit inside
each fish suspended in still water
from the fat red tongue in the living
mouth of war?

We knew, above all, we had to make
friends quickly with the prankster
holding on, riding a crowing white
rooster much bigger than himself.

Throw them into the pit, dump
them all in, the sacks of bones
and baskets of ashes, shovel in
the shards, the dusty chaff, corn
shucks, potsherds, smoking clinkers,
piles of snuffed candle stubs.

In they go, bundles of oily rags
and nappies, caskets of poxy
bedclothes, tattered burlap bags
of spent shells, armless dolls
and wheelless wheelbarrows,
the stripped spokes of slaughtered
umbrellas, everything bulldozed in,
cracked cups and dented kettles,
tarnished brass bells without clappers,
ball joints, steering columns and bent
axles, wagonloads of smoldering
tires, crushed hubcaps, the half
hulls of bottomless boats.

Haul them over and push them in,
carcasses of bedsprings, stained
velvet sofas and overstuffed chairs
spilling stuffing, splintered tables,
smashed pianos, scorched shoes
and burnt brooms, tangles of chains,
handcuffs and busted locks,
buckets of rusty wires, nails, bolts,
leaking batteries, empty paint cans,
frozen hinges and headless hammers.
Up to the edge, over the side,
into the pit, shove them in, all away.

There they go catapulting
and crashing down, a continuous
clattering racket thundering

dust and reeking smoke of tar,
one odd ping of a piano string,
a few brief flames spitting
and hissing, the entire roaring
mischief falling away, down,
dimming, deeper, farther.

A hollow of quiet begins to rise
as the clanking tumult vanishes
into the depths, beyond sight,
beyond sound, maybe beyond
the moon beyond the planets,
maybe beyond motion itself, past
the midway to everything else.
And I know for certain
salvation exists. Beautiful,
blessed pit.

He killed my father, strangled my mother,
held my brother's head under the water
until his fury grew quiet; he plucked
my sister into the void and left her there;
he turned my son into the disappearance
of his own cry. He starved my lover,
the bones in the moonlight. He burned
my whole orchestra to the ground with me
inside and swept the ashes into the gorge.
He could have been madness; he could have been
tumult; he could have been raptor, scavenger,
eclipse; he could have been precipice; he
could have been memory; he could have
been time; he could have been all we ever had.

Wind is especially partial
to the old, the dying and the dead.
It moves among them causing dry
acacia and cassie beans to speak
from their pod-paper caskets. It lifts
the sharp spines of withered
oak leaves and the bony bodies
of their sisters to the edges
of their beds then wanes, fades away
to let them lie again in stillness.

It makes skies of the dust
of the deceased. It makes ragged
moths and raveled grey petals
of airborne ashes. With autumn rain
it urges faltering grasses along
ice-edged marshes to relinquish
at last and abandon their positions.

The wind does not desert
emaciated canyons in their stone
disintegration. It returns again and again
to worn and weathered outcrops
as if rock were god to everything
that wind will never be.

The rasping breath, the halting,
failing rattle, the expiring sigh
are the sounds the wind makes
as it escapes its open cages. Creating
transfiguration simply by departure,
it forges death from life.

The faces of the oldest great-
grandparents are the ancient
designs of the wind made flesh.
Go now to a mirror as to a castle.

Enter there. Notice the structure
of the wind's ways. Let wind speak
its name with wind. Draw your fingers
along the place of the wind's ways,
as you may never touch the wind itself.

Certain pieces of the earth, some
of the sky, can rest on the tip of one
finger—a crust of river snail, the scene
in a seaside sparrow's eye, Venus when
it appears as a grain-of-salt crescent
of light just after dusk, the Great
Wall of China seen from the moon.

Some things lend themselves nicely
to measure by the end of a finger—
a purple fire opal this big, this much
butter, a silence this long. A fingertip
can also suggest a slight summons,
a beckoning of a subtle size. Held high
when wet, a finger can measure the wind.

Yet some occasions are too multiple
to be found and marked by a single
finger—eight blue jays positioned
in a dead tree at eight levels departing
from their sites toward eight stars
of a winter night. And some are too
amorphous—time in the swirl
of an electron cloud.

And many pieces are never conducive
to measurement of any kind—the future
inside the seed of a sea lion bull, the history
inside the egg of a bunch grass lizard,
the knot of space where history and future
cross. A band of neutrinos, possessing
no notice of either birth or loss, passes
clear through without altering at all
life or flesh or fingerbone.

A finger can measure itself, write of its own
stature and soul on sand or walls or paper,
gauge its power, describe its slow demise,
its gradual disappearance, calculate
the full weight of that.

Even though, like a stone sinking
in a night sea, it knows depth
and the heavy cloak of darkness; even
though, like a thundercloud in wind,
it is torn apart and reassembled over
and over; even though it draws in,
pulls its ragged edges close around
its central heart like a blossom
of bindweed at dusk; and even though
its form is as vague and sharp as a shadow
of smoke against a winter hillside;
still it maintains a hard, viable seed
of calm at its core, possesses
the seeking tendency of tendrils

and roots, recalls its lasting kinship
with the past and future wounds
of the living, holds to the heritage
of that certainty, gives itself finally
over to all those powers that rise
by themselves—water oak and willow
saplings, leafy stems of field
thistles, sunflowered and weed-thick
fallows, gatherings of dragonflies,
flockings of warblers, fog in sunlight,
pond turtle and pole star surfacing,
coyote cry of proclamation up
to the moon, and the dominion
of birth, and the kingdom of promise.

In the bobbing of the waterthrush, the trotting
            of the wild boar, in the stiff-legged jogging
of the nine-banded armadillo, the sideways

darting of the desert cottontail
                        and the drumming
                  hind feet of kangaroo rats, in the flight
      of the bluethroat across the Bering Sea,

the floating of the purple sea snail in its raft

            of mucous bubbles, the pouncing of coyote, the springing
                  leap of springbok and springtail,

            the green gangly ascending of treefrog, the burrowing

of the two-gilled bloodworm and the scrambling of the flightless
      tiger beetle, present in the scarlet blooming forth

                  of claret cup cacti,

      in the creeping of morning glory and the winding
                  of kinnickinnick, present
in the gripping of coon oysters to sea whips and to each other,

            in wind drifting the seed of cotton grass, carrying
                  the keys of white ash, the rolling

            of tumbleweed, the sailing of white-tailed kite,
      the gliding of crystal spider on its glassy strand, found
                  in the falling of golden persimmons,

      the dropping of butternuts, pecans, the rooting

of the fragrant roseroot, in the changing colors of the luring
      sargassum fish, the balancing upside down

of the trumpet fish among sea feathers, in the water-skating
of the stilt spider, the soaring of flying fish,
in the climbing, the tumbling, the swinging,

the pirouetting, the vaulting . . . in light in living

motion everywhere it appears, as offering, as evidence,
as recompense.

Here we are, all of us now, some of us
in emerald feathers, in chestnut or purple,
some with bodies of silver, red,
or azure scales, some with faces
of golden fur, some with sea-floating
sails of translucent blue, some pulsing
with fluorescence at dusk, some
pulsing inside shell coverings shining
like obsidian, or inside whorled
and spotted spindle shells, or inside
leaves and petals folded and sealed
like tender shells.

Because many of us have many names—
black-masked or black-footed or blue-
footed, spiny, barbed, whiskered or ringed,
three-toed, nine-banded, four-horned,
whistling or piping, scavenger or prey—
we understand this attribute of god.
Because some of us, not yet found, possess
no names of any kind, we understand,
as well, this attribute of god.

All of us are here, whether wingless
clawless, eyeless, or legless, voiceless,
or motionless, whether hanging
as pods of fur and breath in branches
knitted over the earth or hanging
from stone ceilings in mazes of hallways
beneath the earth, whether blown across
oceans trailing tethers of silk, or taken
off course, caught in storms of thunder
currents or tides of snow, whether free
in cells of honey or free over tundra
plains or alive inside the hearts of living
trees, whether merely moments of inert

binding in the tight blink of buried
eggs, or a grip of watching in the cold
wick of water-swept seeds, this—beyond
faith, beyond doubt—we are here.

Stray cat (one of ten million million
anonymous ordinaries) slinking through
the hedges as if slinking mattered,
you were never designed by great fortune
of the heavens. No god of the beginning
ever commanded, "Let there be forsaken
cat moving belly-to-ground through the ramparts
of these scraggly bushes tonight." No god
took a winter forest of shadows marked
with snow, modeled them specifically
to fashion your pelt. No glad god held
your head in his hands, breathed the soul
of felinity into your own particular nostrils.

Why act as if you knew differently?
No one has anointed you with fanfare
and trumpets. No wise men knelt
beside your blind and squalling birth.
You were never chosen by priests
to have your neck wrung and broken,
your body mummified, wound with cloths,
offered up. And no one desires you now,
not even to butcher or skin you, not
to roast you or feast on your stringy flesh.

Why then prance your case?
Why yowl tonight of your predicament?
What is it among your mass
of molecules and corpuscles, among
the strings and roots and smolder
of old star material composing your presence
that convinces you so thoroughly
of the integrity of your being?

Even in the beauty of your pose
in the shade of summer treetops

or in the preening of the evening sun
on your fur as you lounge beside
the fence, even there you possess no
inherent absolute. What is it that
compels you to hold to the validity
of your heart, a fact in fact defining
exactly what you are?

I watch your unwavering watch
of the night's flickering slips and claws
and raw earthly realignments, your fierce
and wary, your very own, the daring
lie of your fiery green eyes.

Though it may appear that this wayward
stumbling is errant, choreographers
can see that it possesses the same grace
as a leaf fallen into concert with a steady
creek and its swerving current of rapids.

Though the progress of this thought
might sound to some like stuttering,
the listening blind know that it follows
the same pattern as rain streaming
in gusts against a windowpane at night.

Though the story may occasionally
become dizzy and its cadence sporadic,
the hero of the tale spins with it
naturally like a funnel of dust across
a prairie, faltering, regaining.

The twisting and weaving of a pea vine
intertwining with its invisible love
may appear to be without direction
or purpose, but students of tenacity
and sunlight know better.

So this sudden ceasing,
this vanishing, might be called
death by some who are watching,
as with a shift of vision a tree
near at hand vanishes into the forest
surrounding. Yet any witness born
to the vagaries of wildwoods
will see the same single being
still present and undiminished.

One way it's done is by a self-dividing
black seam showing itself across the sphere
of a cave swallow's brown-spotted pink egg,
the splintered cracking commencing,
the shell and its form falling further,
splitting into thin shards like a skim
of ice parceling over shallow mud in March.

Yet this tracery of shattering
shell itself has a form in lines
I could draw with one hand, take apart
again with the other.

Or breaking an old form
might be like lifting the naked
network of a spring sycamore explicitly
out of the field, moving it straight
into the body, creating a new union
thereby of branching bone-twigs
in the breast, an arboreal tangle
of sustenance in the blood-rooting
vessels of the breast, the old ways
of grief or joy in the breast breaking open
like the red softness of buds in April.
Even the habitual breathing
of April itself could be paced anew
by this repositioning.

Is the decrepit pattern of winter
realigned when two eagles, screeching,
feathers erect, clasp claws mid-heaven,
latch and fall, spinning together
momentarily upside down inside
a harsh, grey wind of snow?

This very question might be broken also
into pieces by the piercings of a thousand
perfectly aimed summer stars demolishing
immediately any winter drama.

If the old form of death could be fully
understood—a form like naked claws
latching together mid-breath, a structure
of falling like furled ice closing
around the blood of a red blossom—
then someone might break death apart too
with a thousand lines aimed perfectly
at the welds of its network. Or someone
might simply shatter its structure
by lifting it carefully with one hand,
moving it, as if by love, right into the body
with the other, its decrepit habits
taken in, encompassed anew, surprised
by this endearment, coaxed to yield
to such a gentle form of union.

It existed before all the paper bells
fell with their shivered ringing
from the river trees; before
the ground apples turned
to sweet pudding for the honey
ants and the titbirds; before the fog
returned the sea to the sun.

Far away in the distance, it was
outside a tumbleweed tacking
its wobbled way eastward;
outside a kerchief on the line
rolling its white like a wave
coming ashore; before the wild-
eyed horse on the carousel
faced the first round of evening;
outside and before bitter ginger
or Ceylon cinnamon or the Valencia
orange; before any orange at all
was peeled, sectioned, shared.

The precedent was charted before
there were metallic wood-boring
beetle paths, or comet paths,
or vole paths hollowed deep
in the blue beneath the snow
of the field; before the dirt tunnel
and tower of termite paths,
or the liquid weave of a snail path
over the rubbish path of the forest
trail, or the path of a desert rain
leaving in its wake blooming
mariola, buzzing green toads, marble-
wings over violet blossoms.

It was reckoned before all
the void of static stars became
spilling stars, luminous with motion,
occupant and audible with measure,
long before this particular thought
of pity when not was everything
and was not. The precedent was there
within that absence whose only place
is imagination, whose only hope
is its only place.

Come up out of the river. Walk out
the way fog walks, without significance,
enfolding everything, claiming nothing,
like the gold of a green brier thicket
in the dawn claims nothing from the soul.

Come up out of the deep, water
spilling off your body like dissolving
pieces of silver bone, beyond bone,
beyond silver, the steel skeleton
of sorrow dissolving to rain.

Even the coho, even the sockeye rise,
though tethered forever in river
heaves and yelps.

Walk out of the river fire, the radiances
of your body falling as you come,
like spears of burning oil and spikes
falling from a flaming pine. Burn
like water burns in a noonday sun.

Even the cypress, even the bulrushes
rise from water, though they are as bound
as stone moon craters to the earth.

Come like the river comes, voluptuous
with sky, broken and mended again
by the breaking. Walk out the way the plum
walks from its blossom, ravaging
with transfiguration, killing in the way
a seed always kills.

Sentient as script, come up out of the river
like *river*. Come the way the savior as *water*
keeps rising out of the water, keeps walking
closer and closer as *sea* to the sea.

Come. Now. You are the one
who understands the way.

acknowledgments

My gratitude to the editors of the following
publications in which some of the poems in this volume first
appeared, some in slightly different forms and two with different titles.

The Antioch Review: Generations; Into Their Own

Boston Review: Jacob's Ladder

Crazyhorse: The Match

eleventhMuse: Mischief in the Madrigal

Field: Alpha and Omega; A Statement of Certainty; A Traversing

The Georgia Review: In General

The Gettysburg Review: A Meeting of the Ways;
The History of Starlight at Night

The Hudson Review: Come, Drink Here

Iron Horse Literary Review: Symbols and Signs; Into the Wind's Castle;
The Questing; Seeing What Is Seen

North Dakota Quarterly: This Little Glade, Remember;
The Measure of a Finger

onEarth: Tabula Rasa

Orion Online: Grief

Poetry: The Body and the Soul; God and His People; The Passing of the
Wise Men; Keeping Up; Feeding Our Ancient Ancestors;
Servant, Birthright

Portland: Where God's Grief Appears

Potpourri: The Soul of Subtlety

Prairie Schooner: Bearings on a Winter Evening

River City: And Motion in Philosophy

Spirituality and Health: Who Might Have Said

Tampa Review: Creating a Pillar to Heaven

The Tin House: Study from Right Angles; The Lost Creation of the Earth

Wabash Magazine: On the Eve of the Hearing

Thanks to Robert Lewis for first bringing to my attention
Heterocephalus glaber.

Pattiann Rogers has published eight books of poetry, a book-length essay, *The Dream of the Marsh Wren*, and *A Covenant of Seasons*, poems and monotypes, in collaboration with the artist Joellyn Duesberry. *Song of the World Becoming: New and Collected Poems, 1981–2001* was a finalist for the *Los Angeles Times* Book Prize and an Editor's Choice in *Booklist*. *Firekeeper: New and Selected Poems* was a finalist for the Lenore Marshall Award and a *Publishers Weekly* Best Book of 1994. Rogers is the recipient of two NEA Grants, a Guggenheim Fellowship, and a Poetry Fellowship from the Lannan Foundation. Her poems have won the Tietjens Prize, the Hokin Prize, and the Bock Prize from *Poetry*; the Roethke Prize from *Poetry Northwest*; two Strousse Awards from *Prairie Schooner*; and five Pushcart Prizes. Her papers are archived in the Sowell Family Collection of Literature, Community, and the Natural World at Texas Tech University. Rogers has been a visiting writer at numerous universities and colleges and was associate professor at the University of Arkansas from 1993 to 1997. She is the mother of two sons and two grandsons and lives with her husband, a retired geophysicist, in Colorado.

PENGUIN POETS

TED BERRIGAN
Selected Poems
The Sonnets

PHILIP BOOTH
Lifelines

JIM CARROLL
Fear of Dreaming
Void of Course

BARBARA CULLY
Desire Reclining

CARL DENNIS
New and Selected Poems
  1974–2004
Practical Gods

DIANE DI PRIMA
Loba

STUART DISCHELL
Dig Safe

STEPHEN DOBYNS
Pallbearers Envying the
  One Who Rides
The Porcupine's Kisses

ROGER FANNING
Homesick

AMY GERSTLER
Crown of Weeds
Ghost Girl
Medicine
Nerve Storm

DEBORA GREGER
Desert Fathers, Uranium
  Daughters
God

ROBERT HUNTER
Sentinel

BARBARA JORDAN
Trace Elements

MARY KARR
Viper Run

JACK KEROUAC
Book of Blues
Book of Haikus

JOANNE KYGER
As Ever

ANN LAUTERBACH
If in Time
On a Stair

PHYLLIS LEVIN
Mercury

WILLIAM LOGAN
Macbeth in Venice
Night Battle
Vain Empires

DEREK MAHON
Selected Poems

MICHAEL McCLURE
Huge Dreams: Sun
  Francisco and Beat
  Poems

CAROL MUSKE
An Octave Above Thunder

ALICE NOTLEY
The Descent of Alette
Disobedience
Mysteries of Small Houses

LAWRENCE RAAB
The Probable World
Visible Signs

PATTIANN ROGERS
Generations

STEPHANIE STRICKLAND
V

ANNE WALDMAN
Kill or Cure
Marriage: A Sentence

PHILIP WHALEN
Overtime: Selected Poems

ROBERT WRIGLEY
Lives of the Animals
Reign of Snakes

JOHN YAU
Borrowed Love Poems